Dear Liar

Mrs. Patrick Campbell as Eliza Doolittle in *Pygmalion*, and Bernard Shaw in 1912, the year he wrote *Pygmalion*

Dear Liar

A COMEDY OF LETTERS ADAPTED BY

Jerome Kilty

FROM THE CORRESPONDENCE OF

Bernard Shaw

AND

Mrs. Patrick Campbell

DODD, MEAD & COMPANY

NEW YORK · 1960

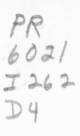

PR
6021
I 262
D 4

This Adaptation Copyright © 1960 by Jerome Kilty

Extracts from PYGMALION, Copyright 1916 (Renewed 1944) 1930, 1942, by G. Bernard Shaw and THE APPLE CART, Copyright © 1930 by G. Bernard Shaw, Renewed © 1957 The Public Trustee as Executor of the Estate of G. Bernard Shaw, are reprinted by permission of the Public Trustee and the Society of Authors.

The correspondence of Bernard Shaw and Mrs. Patrick Campbell was originally published in BERNARD SHAW AND MRS. PATRICK CAMPBELL: THEIR CORRESPONDENCE, Ed. by Alan Dent. Copyright 1952 by Alfred A. Knopf, Inc., New York.

Mr. Kilty would like to express his gratitude to Alan Dent whose editing of the correspondence between Bernard Shaw and Mrs. Patrick Campbell has helped immeasurably in the preparation of this "Comedy of Letters."

Library of Congress Catalog Card Number: 60-14154
Printed in the United States of America
by Vail-Ballou Press, Inc., Binghamton, N. Y.

Note on the Play

There are only the two characters; the actor who speaks the words of G.B.S. and the actress who speaks those of Mrs. Patrick Campbell. He is dressed in a dark, semi-formal suit or perhaps a smoking jacket. Whatever seems best for the particular actor playing the role. She would have three lovely evening dresses that are at once "modern" and "period." Again, they should be designed to show the actress off as beautifully as possible. No attempt should be made to represent the features either of Shaw or Mrs. Campbell. A touch of Irish accent, in English-speaking countries, should be used by Shaw. She will wear one dress in the first act, one in the first part of the second, and another after she returns to the stage for the last part of the play. The last dress should be the simplest of all and should be designed to help the actress feel older than she was at the beginning.

The set is very simple. A lovely writing desk for her with a feminine and charming small armchair before it. A small footstool is under the desk. He will have a standing desk with an appropriate high stool in front of it and, down right of the desk, a small chair or hassock which can be easily carried about. In the middle of the stage is a practical hatbox with a hinged top standing on a small, light table. There should be an entrance up center and a French window behind her desk stage left. The desks are placed to face diagonally outward so the actors will have freedom to move about the center of the stage.

Act 1 covers the period from 1899 to 1914; Act 2, from 1914 to 1939.

Dear Liar

Act One

Curtain.

The ACTOR *and* ACTRESS *are discovered on stage. Between them is hatbox, closed.*

ACTRESS [*to the audience*] Good evening. For forty years of their very public lives there existed a very private and infinitely intriguing relationship between the famous English actress, Mrs. Patrick Campbell, and the well-known vegetarian *and* playwright, George Bernard Shaw. When Mr. Shaw was, as he said himself, old enough to know better, he fell head over heels in love with Mrs. Campbell. He dreamed he walked on air; he ran singing through the streets to meet her, his Stella Stellarum, his glorious white marble lady, his Beatricissima. His love, he said, was everlasting and undying.

ACTOR [*to audience*] But forty years later, when he

heard of her death, Shaw wrote [*He unfolds news-paper and reads from it*] "Everyone is greatly relieved, herself, I should think, most of all, for she could not live with real people in the real world. Still she was a great enchantress, and she enchanted me, among the rest." [*He folds up newspaper*] This is the story of that enchantment told in their own words in the hundreds of letters they sent to one another over the years, letters which they both saved, fought over; returned to each other and very nearly lost in the second world war.

ACTRESS [*to audience*] In 1940 "Mrs. Pat," as she was known to the public, died in the South of France. With her were all the letters which she kept in this hatbox, under her bed. The English lady who buried her left everything else behind and managed to get the hatbox over to England just five days before the Germans were in Paris.

ACTOR [*to audience*] But it is forty years earlier that our story begins. [*They open the hatbox together*] Imagine, if you will, the end of the last century. Victoria is on the throne; England the most modern of modern nations; Mrs. Patrick Campbell is at the peak of her career. Bernard Shaw was ending his career as a music and drama critic and was beginning to turn out plays of his own, none of them achieving much success.

[*Actress takes both packets of letters out of the hat-box and begins to leaf through them*] Inspired by the beauty and artistry of Mrs. Campbell in *The Second Mrs. Tanqueray*, he began work on a new play, *Caesar and Cleopatra*, hoping that she might act in it when it was finished. With this in mind, he invited her down to his cottage in Hindhead for a week-end visit and—

ACTRESS. But it is all here, in the letters. [*Handing him his packet*] Will you begin please, Mr. Shaw?

SHAW [*takes letters*] With pleasure, Mrs. Campbell.

They each cross to their desks. As SHAW *recites his first letter,* CAMPBELL *begins by holding a single letter as if she is just reading it.*

SHAW. Blen Cathra Hindhead, 12th of April, 1899. Dear Mrs. Patrick Campbell [*He looks at her while he speaks. She has her back turned to him*] We have this house until the 14th May only; so come quickly. Mrs. Shaw will be delighted to see you. The vegetables have triumphed over their traducers. I was told that my meatless diet was so poor that I could not repair the bones that were broken in my foot. So I have just had an Xradiograph taken and lo! perfectly mended bone so beautifully white that I have left instructions that, if I die, a glove stretcher is to be made out of them and sent to you as a souvenir. [MRS. CAMPBELL *laughs; puts letter down, sits and listens*] I have seen your latest photograph. Wonderful as it is, I would have photographed you in bed, saying, "It's tempting Providence." After all, there are lots of beautiful people about, but they can't all take a filament of gray matter from their brains and thread it through the hole in the dramatist's needle. It is your power to do that that is the real gift. I do hope you can come. Yours sincerely, George Bernard Shaw.

SHAW *reads from a single letter as she speaks. This is only to establish the convention; it is not constantly repeated.*

CAMPBELL. 33 Kensington Sq. W. 21 April, 1899. My dear Mr. Shaw: I dread seeing my photographs— the days of dewlaps have arrived! God help me and all women! I am afraid I won't be able to accept your invitation. Oh, that I had mislaid countless sons and daughters and that they would all turn up today or tomorrow and prevent me accepting an offer to tour in America—twenty weeks at so many dollars a minute! I've been asked to appear in Rostand's wonderful fairy play. Wouldn't it be nice if you "Englished" it for us? Do let me know. May God bless you for the smiles you make us smile and forgive you for those literary lack-of-taste misdemeanors that make us squirm. Yours sincerely, Beatrice Stella Campbell.

SHAW. Dear Mrs. Patrick Campbell: I don't think it would do for me to meddle with Rostand's fairy scheme; it would give it a flavor of brimstone at once. No. Give your contemporaries a chance. Turn to the rising suns. I am exhausted, hackneyed, vulgarized, and far too old for these games: forty-five last July as ever was. [*During this he carries hatbox and stand upstage center where it remains*] Yours sincerely, G. Bernard Shaw.

CAMPBELL [*to audience*] In the fifth month of the new century my husband was killed in the fighting in South Africa. We had been married for sixteen years and the loneliness was overwhelming. The only thing was to plunge back into my work and within a year I had opened in a new play.

SHAW. 7th November, 1901. My dear Mrs. Patrick Campbell: I finally secured a seat to your performance. It was really a great achievement and the use of Handel's music was a fine touch. I do, however, think the "Hallelujah Chorus" might be improved by steeping in boiling water for ten minutes or so. Oh, yes! It is not natural that your leading man should die unassisted the way he does, especially after gurgling like Othello with his throat cut. However, all that is nothing. The impression was overwhelming. Yours enthusiastically, Bernard Shaw.

CAMPBELL [*to audience*] After this I appeared in a series of wonderful plays, one success after another; *Pelleas and Melisande, Hedda Gabler* and *Bella Donna,* which I took back and forth between England and America. It was some years before I heard from Mr. Shaw again. My children were growing up and already getting married; my son, Beo, in 1909 and my daughter, Stella, in 1911.

SHAW [*to audience*] And I was turning out one play after another. *Fanny's First Play* was a walloping success, running for 600 performances and began to bring in money such as I'd never seen before. After this had opened, I set to work in earnest on a play I'd long planned for Mrs. Campbell—*Pygmalion*—and early in 1911 it was finished. [*To Campbell*] Dear Mrs. Campbell: I have just heard of your return from America. As it happens, I shall be in your neighborhood tomorrow afternoon. And . . . and . . . Might I drop in for tea?

CAMPBELL [*to audience*] Before I had time to reply, the doorbell rang and he bounded into my sitting room in Kensington Square and I was listening to him read his new play and aghast at the unpleasant sounds of Eliza's cockney accent coming out of his mouth. When he'd finished, he said he'd written the play for me—and he left. I wanted to thank him—but I couldn't appear too eager. I wrote— [*To Shaw*] My dear Mr. Shaw: First of all, my thanks for letting me hear the play and for thinking I can be your pretty slut. I wonder if I could please you? Still, I must admit that it was a great pleasure—and such a surprise —for me to see you again.

SHAW. Stella! I was afraid you'd see through it. But I could think of no other way to get you to hear it to the end. Then, when you said those inelegant words, I was sure it was all up—that you'd never be my little flower girl.

CAMPBELL. I didn't say anything at all. Of course, I saw through it. Don't you remember? As soon as you'd finished the first scene [*She rises and walks toward him*] I rose and said, "You beast! You wrote this for me, every line of it. I can hear you mimicking my voice in it!" That's *all* I said. But if you're really in earnest the next step is to tell me what the business proposal is—when, where and with whom and *perhaps* one day I will . . . Oh, never mind. Come. [*She comes down and speaks quickly to audience*] And he arrived for tea on a glorious June afternoon with laughter in his eyes and a contract in his pocket. When he went away, I had the strange impression that our friendship was ripening perhaps *too* rapidly; when I received his next note I was certain of it. I caught him in the act of slipping it under the door.

She crosses up and looks out window through next speech.

SHAW [*he walks toward her*] You knew it would happen! I went calmly to your house to discuss business with you, as hard as nails, and as I am a living man, I fell head over heels in love with you in the first thirty seconds. How long did it last? For thirty hours! Why, I dreamed and walked on air all the following afternoon just as if my next birthday were my twentieth.

CAMPBELL. But you are not twenty and the theater is business . . . a very big business! If, I tell you, *if*, I can get the right people together to do it I will be your pretty slut. That far I will go. As for walking on air, the clouds have two sides to them, and who is to say on which side either of us is walking?

SHAW [*he crosses stage right of desk, away from her*] Very well, then, to business. I am going to break the shattering news that you have captured me . . . for your own theater! You see! That is the worst of having anything to do with me: you are dragged at once into the brazen atmosphere behind which my poor timid little soul hides and cowers and dreams. Your plans will be known to everyone before this letter reaches you, with a romantic glamor round them, but still sufficiently correct to make it necessary for you to play with your cards on the table. So beware!

CAMPBELL [coming down to him] I always play with my cards on the table, not in my pocket. That was your game. All that pretense of "being in the neighborhood."

SHAW [crossing toward her. They meet center] A perfectly respectable ruse. What's the matter? Are you afraid you might involve your heart with this unregenerate socialist and actor . . . as he has with you? Or are you afraid you won't?

CAMPBELL. Beatrice Webb is right, you are a sprite. And how can one fall in love with a sprite? Will you come on Friday and I promise we can be alone!

She goes and looks through window in a romantic mood.

SHAW [to audience] If Stella wanted to capture you you might as well go willingly, for she was irresistible. All of London knew her charms from across the footlights but I was learning about them from a much different perspective. I would not have believed I had that left in me. [To Campbell] Dear Stella: many thanks for Friday; and for a Saturday of delightful dreams back up in the clouds. I am all right now, though, down on earth again with all my cymbals and side drums and "blaring vulgarities" in full blast; but it would be meanly cowardly to pretend that you are not a very wonderful lady, or that the spell did not work most enchantingly on me for fully twelve hours. G.B.S.

CAMPBELL. Shall we keep to business, Mr. Shaw? I have made a formal offer for the theater and have let the world know that I am going into management and that I may act in Mr. Shaw's Eliza. [*Crossing to desk where she sits at end of speech*] Perhaps you have already seen it in the papers. Who will play the part opposite to me of Henry Higgins, I don't know yet, but never mind. We will find someone.

SHAW. Beatricissima: I have just seen it in the papers! and I am going to be horrid, and I have a frightful headache—so pity me. I wonder how your dentist manages? He *must* love you—and yet he can't always help hurting you—deliberately and scientifically hurting you. *I* should plunge a knife into my heart and die at your feet. Yet I am going to pull half your teeth out, without gas. I proceed in my professional literary manner. Hear the essayist. [*She starts to speak. He stops her*] Silence. O Stella Stellarum, there is nothing more certain in the process of the suns than that if you attempt management on the single-star system, nothing—not even my genius added to your own—can save you from final defeat. "Male and female created He them." Your public is more than half feminine: you cannot satisfy their longing for a male to idealize; and how can they idealize a poor salaried employee pushed into a corner and played off the stage? Do you want to be a Duse? A hammer without an anvil? A Sandow playing with paper dumbbells! Produce *Pygmalion* with a £20 Higgins, and you will have an uproarious success. But the house will be under £200. At the end of a few weeks, the business will stagger. You will be terrified, and will spend wildly on advertisements. You will drop to £120. You will take *Pygmalion* off and draw away from me. You will struggle on until you have lost every farthing; and then it will be America, with all its horrors, to recoup yourself, and the provinces, or retirement, for the rest of your life, like Mrs. Kendal. Talk of Mrs. Tanqueray looking into her mirror; how do you feel now? Now, where am I to find a man to stand up to you on the stage? You are happy playing with worms. Worms never give any trouble; and in plays which can be *produced*, they make the best casts. But my plays must be acted, and acted hard. Who, then, is to be your complement? The John Drew to your Ada Rehan, the Irving to your Ellen Terry? No, Stella! I *must* have a heroic Higgins. And I must not ruin you. Nor myself. I could not love thee, dear, so much, loved I not money more!

CAMPBELL. Oh, Mr. Shaw, you're such a clown! I think I'll call you "Joey"—"Joey the Clown." I know only too well that a two-star show is better than a one-star and that an all-star show is fit only for kings and queens.

SHAW. If you know that why are you being so difficult?

CAMPBELL. I'm not being difficult. If you don't care if I'm happy in my work, there are many that do. James Barrie has a new play for me and Charles Frohman offers me a fortune to take it to America!

SHAW. Yes, yes, I know all about that but for the love of God, Stella, you must be reasonable.

CAMPBELL. I feel thoroughly unreasonable and uncomfortable haggling with you this way. If Higgins is a more important part than Eliza then get a male star and I'll step out.

SHAW. Stella, talk sense! You an established star, a veteran, in fact, must have an established star to play opposite you.

CAMPBELL. A veteran! How dare you! I'm not a veteran! Veteran! That makes me feel like the horse that once won the Derby and has been put out to pasture ever since. A veteran! One would think that my hair's a wig, my eyes are glass and my legs wooden. Well, I've got my eyes, my hair's my own and my legs

are as good as the best! And I *won't* be a day over
thirty-nine! Of course, I do have a daughter who's
twenty-eight, but what of that? It happens in India
all the time.

SHAW. Have you finished?

CAMPBELL. No, I have not. I was told today that you
only wanted me to play Eliza for the joy of making a
fool of me, so everyone can say, "the joke, the enormous joke" of my playing a girl! Well, we'll see who
has the last laugh. I wonder what your nonsensical
play would be without me! I suppose you would like
to know what theater we'll be playing in and the fi-
nancial strength of the undertaking. This, of course,
will be put before you and you will be discreet!

She crosses around desk, stage left, and goes up.

SHAW. I don't want anything put before me. I am an
artist and don't understand finance. I want my Liza
and no other Liza. I wrote the play to have my Liza.
And I must have a proper Higgins *for* my Liza. I won't
listen to reason. [*He crosses to chair and sits*] I will sit
here and howl. I can howl for twenty years, getting
louder and louder all the time. All I ask is to have my
own way in everything!

CAMPBELL. Oh, darling, what a letter! I call you
"darling" because "dear Mr. Shaw" means nothing at
all—whilst darling means most dear and most dear

means a man, and a mind and a speaking—such as you and your mind and your speech! I long to get on with the whole thing and call rehearsals on Sept. 1st.

SHAW. September 1st is agreeable to me if we find the right Higgins. I will not budge from this position. Our friends are beginning to talk. Cartloads of chaff are falling on me like snow on Mont Blanc. Mrs. Shaw and I were with James Barrie on Monday night. At eleven I rose to go. Barrie said in his slowest Scotch manner, "Shall you be seeing Mrs. Campbell again tonicht?" Such is the ribaldry I have brought on you. I wish I could fall in love without telling everybody. I shall be fifty-six on the twenty-sixth of this month, and I have not yet grown up. [*Stands*] I must go now and read this letter to my wife, Charlotte. [*Crosses up to desk*] My love affairs are her unfailing amusement. Besides, I love an audience. Oh, forgive this blasphemy; but my head is still bad and it makes me naughty—Stella, September 1st—yes?

CAMPBELL. September 1st—yes.

SHAW [*to audience*] But it was not to be, not yet. A few weeks later, shortly after I'd begun my annual holiday on the Continent, Stella was involved in a horrible taxicab accident [CAMPBELL *pulls footstool from under desk and puts feet on it*] which brought our plans to a crashing halt and kept her from acting for more than a year. She was driving to the Albert Hall, holding on her lap her ever-present Pekinese, this one named Georgina.

SHAW *sits on high stool.*

CAMPBELL. It was a blinding bang!—my head rose six inches and then the hemorrhage came down my face under the skin, and I have been a sight of sights ever since with aches and pains in every inch of me and bruises as large as saucers—I'm afraid I can't play Bella Donna again—it must close— Nor Liza now, I fear. May Strachey begged me to write and say it would be grand and that you rather owed it to me— to let us have Liza to take with us on the rest cure in France. I can read to her—what the world will never hear now and we would let no other soul see it. Write and make me get well. A letter a day won't be enough.

During her illness, they do not look directly at each other. There should be a sense of "distance" here.

SHAW. Hotel de Russie, Bad Kissingen. 9th August 1912. Stella, Stella: all the winds of the north are musical with the thousand letters I have written to you on this holiday. But at last the car's gears got jammed at the fall of evening: and as I live (by vegetables)! I *stood*—stood on my straining legs on that hillside for ten hours, keeping up the spirits of my chauffeur whilst he took the whole transmission to pieces and put it together again. I found a village and a clean double-bedded room in a *Gasthaus* for Charlotte and her sister, and they slept happily. I and the chauffeur kept up magnificently and greeted the dawn with the exultation of men who had not turned a hair. And that day we did not turn many hairs. But the next (which was yesterday)—my word! I tell you, my good woman, that if you expect to find any romantic nonsense about me, you are greatly mistaken. My knees are out of order: my calves are like a shop assistant's where there are no seats behind the counter. I shall not feel romantic about you again for at least ten minutes. Yes— I will send you a rough proof of *Pygmalion*. I warn you beforehand, however, that if you read it again you are lost; you will be at my feet at once with your dark hair looking dyed because of the gleaming of my brown shoes through the roots. If you by any chance leave France before the end of the month, let me know. Charlotte will be here all the time. She gasps in rarefied air, whilst her sister wallows in mud at five marks per gasp and per wallow. Neither of them, by the way, is in the least ill; but Charlotte wants to get thin, and her sister wants to get plump; so they both agreed to be asthmatic and have treatments. I have taken the waters myself—one mouthful, which will suffice for the rest of my life. Is it Lady Strachey you are with? If it is, what will she think of me when you trail your victim before her? I solemnly protest that when I went into your house in Kensington Square I was a man of iron, insolently confident in my impenetrability. And in thirty seconds—oh Stella, if you had a rag of decency it *couldn't* have happened. Is this dignified? Is it sensible? At my age—a driveller— a dotard! I will conquer this weakness, or better still trade in it and write plays about it.

CAMPBELL. Write plays about whatever you wish but not, please, about us! My daughter, Stella, when she was little, used to sing a song which she thought was funny. It began like this:

> He's mad, mad, mad,
> He's clean gone off his nut
> He cleans his boots with strawberry jam
> He eats his hat whenever he can
> He's mad—

It's really about you. [*She suddenly moves her head too quickly, giving it a painful twinge*] I still have two black eyes and some screwlike pains in my shoulder.

SHAW. Your mention of Stellinetta reminds me of a time I puzzled her with a piece of Irish folly. We were sitting in the front of a box at the Savoy at some idiotic performance of *Arms and the Man*; and the audience gave me a sort of ovation at the end. My impulse was to rise and bless them [*He makes an elaborate cross in the air*]—it's true I often feel like a Pope. But I didn't. She thought I was cracked, poor infant!

CAMPBELL. You seem to be having a merry time. I wish I were with you but they won't even let me sit up for more than an hour at a stretch. Not to speak of motoring! Here at Aix I am looking at a glorious world, when I look up—and out—but the scullery maids in their pearls and fashions with their bloody nails and sealing-wax lips make my hair stand on end. I have never been to a fashionable cure place before—I am a little astounded. "Laugh and the world laughs with you, snore and you sleep alone." Perhaps some day, if you are very good and behave properly at rehearsal I will write you a love letter.

SHAW. A love letter! *Sancta simplicitas!* When did you ever write me anything else? No; let me write; and do you *pray* for us both; for there is always danger when that devilment Love is at work! Ah! I wish you were with me, you'd keep me out of pickles such as I got into yesterday. Briefly: in a townlet some twenty miles from the French border, the car ruptured a vital organ. So, to get some quiet and avoid being run over in absence of mind, I went into a barber's, forgetting that I'd had my hair cut only the day before, with the result that I am now mowed all but bald. I did not wake up to what was happening until the man started on my eyebrow, probably mistaking it for a supplementary moustache because it turns up at the end in the Mephistophelean manner. As it is, I am cropped to the white, like a fox terrier. I shall not feel romantic about you again for at least ten minutes. If the sun is shining in Savoy, and you are motoring much, ask the chauffeur to give you some lubricating oil to rub on your countenance. If you don't, it will peel. *I* use a skin food; but engine oil is cheaper and equally effective.

CAMPBELL. You don't deserve to be as clever as you are and it's not that you are *so* clever—it's just your exuberant and mischievous mind. I cannot keep up the exuberance like you, and the beloved Irish accent, which I believe the serpent had or Eve would never have noticed the apple, far less eat it. Do something quickly or I shall have vanished. I am so ill! Please!

SHAW. Nonsense! I never encourage illness. My wife is ill; my mother is ill; I am rehearsing two plays simultaneously; and if an earthquake swallowed half the habitable globe, I think I should only laugh. Anyhow, it is I who need sympathy. I have just had a letter from a suffragette beginning, "Poor, ill-used darling . . ." No! You get up and console *me*.

CAMPBELL. Well, darling, I'm not in Heaven, neither have I sixteen chins and what bosom is left me is still straightened. The great genius, James Barrie, who lives opposite you, and whose one-act plays *are* a success, came to see me yesterday and didn't look at me with horror. Do hurry back. I miss you dreadfully—and Liza too.

SHAW. Nearer my goddess to thee by another one hundred and twenty miles. Strangely enough I have never been here in Orleans before. I should like to do a Joan of Arc play some day, beginning with the sweeping up of the cinders after her martyrdom and going on with her arrival in Heaven. One of my scenes will be Voltaire and Shakespeare running down side streets to avoid meeting her. Would you like to play the Maid? You would come in on horseback in shining armor and fight innumerable supers!

CAMPBELL. Your letters are a carnival of words. How can I answer with my poor whining beggars? It will be dreadful when you realize the commonplace, witless charwoman I really am. And you with so many "great women" about you now, Saint Joan and all. If you are back next Monday or Tuesday, will you come at four o'clock and make me laugh and convince me it's worthwhile getting well?

SHAW. Alas, although I am back in England I shall

not be within reach of you on Monday or Tuesday. I have to go up to Liverpool and see them through another rehearsal of *Caesar and Cleopatra*. It was a specially disastrous dress rehearsal. Such dryings-up and wrong cues were never heard. To my taste the climax was reached when the end of the fourth act was approaching and the stage was darkened for the discovery of the murdered Ftatateeta. Cleopatra said "It is dark and I am lonely" with such convincing naturalness that the sympathetic electrician consoled her instantly with a floodlight which deluged the stage.

CAMPBELL. Oh, darling! It's too late to do anything but *accept* you and *love* you—but when you were quite a little boy somebody ought to have said "hush" just once.

SHAW. O glorious white marble lady. What was done to me in my childhood was nothing at all of an intentional kind. I wasn't spoiled; and I wasn't helped. Nobody forbade me to discover what I could of the world's wonders. I was taken for what I was; a disagreeable little beast. Nobody concerned himself or herself as to what I was capable of becoming, nor did I. I did not know I was different from other people (except for the worse). I have discovered all my powers from the outside, with incredulous astonishment, or rather I have discovered that everybody else hasn't got them. My shyness and cowardice have been beyond all belief.

CAMPBELL. Three times yesterday I tried to write, and my temperature has gone up to the moon! Be patient with me. I have been a widow for twelve years and a grandmother for four days and within the last few weeks I nearly gave life the slip. What's that about "shy" and a "coward"—I see you—as sensitive as Keats —as timid as a lamb—and that "want of taste" we grumbled at, is a sort of swank. These letters of yours are traps—traps like your Irish accent.

SHAW. Oh! You are right! Shut your ears tight against this blarneying Irish liar and actor. He will fill his fountain pen with your heart's blood, and sell your most sacred emotions on the stage. He will! He is a writing and talking machine that has worked for nearly forty years until its skill is devilish. I should have warned you before; but I thought his white hairs and fifty-six years had made his philandering ridiculous, and now it is too late.

CAMPBELL. There is a tract called *Led on Step by Step!* That's what's happening to me. You didn't *really* think that I believed you came to see me because you were interested in *me*. I knew it was Liza and I was delighted that you should be so businesslike in such a bewilderingly charming way—I haven't said "kiss me" because life is too short for the kiss my heart calls for. Look into my eyes for two minutes without speaking if you dare! Then how many hours would you be late for dinner?

SHAW. If I looked into your eyes without speaking for two minutes (silent for two minutes with an audience even of one! Impossible, cried the fiend) I might see heaven. I think you are getting well. I hear a ring. I see a flash! The able, courageous Stella is stirring. Stella! Who is Stella? A woman, well, can she love a human dredger? That's what I am! Does she want to clasp brass to her bosom—oh, her bosom! I remember now—the jade!—when she first took my hand she shook it so that it touched her bosom, an infamous abandoned trick; it thrilled through me, through all my brass for hours. I was young and foolish then and could be thrilled. What did she care for me then? What was my knuckle to her—it caught me just on the knuckle. Had she felt what I felt she would have risen up into the skies and set me there at her right hand. Oh, you must, you must be torn out of your bed and shaken into rude health. Or else I will get into the bed myself and we shall perish together scandalously.

CAMPBELL. There are parts of your letters I cannot reply to, except by golden silence. Did I once call you a clown? I expect it was when you said "I am God."

This week is going to be a bad week—they tell me I'm
to be operated on at last—I won't be able to write for
a few days—my friends must fold their hands for me
—I am glad we met. Good-night.

SHAW. Shall I tell you the calculations I have been
going over in my head ever since you became ill?
Listen. Money. She must have money to go on with.
Has she any? Let me see. £116 a week all through the
run of *Bella Donna*. Half to the bankers to pay off
debts. That leaves £58 a week going to her credit. But
it also proves that the bankers must have allowed her
to overdraw recklessly. But there is a limit to all over-
drafts. That limit may be approaching—may be already reached! Are there friends—for pride is no use;
when you *must* have money you must take it or raise
it—must, must, must, must, *must!* DD—Savile—who
is there? But if they didn't offer and insist she might
go to a moneylender. She would. Delicacy: that's the
difficulty; a woman is visibly spending money like
water and earning nothing; and people talk of delicacy!
Thank God I have no delicacy—no good taste—she
said so—oh, sweet revenge, to turn myself, like Jupiter
with Danaë, into a shower of gold! Only, I haven't gold
enough; I'm not rich and I'm a member of a firm:
Charlotte & Company. No; it doesn't run to a shower.
How much will she need? No; I must be prudent; how

little can she scrape through with? There's the rent, the Christmas quarter. Then Christmas boxes, bills, nurses, doctors. Of course she is saving a lot by being in bed; no dressing up, no taxis. Would £250 get her over it? Oh, God! To offer Stella a filthy little £250! I spit on myself. But she says she can't keep money—despicable weakness! Better perhaps dole out a little at a time; other fortnights will follow Christmas. How much can I afford? Ass! why ask that question over and over again? You know perfectly well that you want to give her a thousand pounds. Very well: put your check book in your pocket and go to her and ask her. If she does *not* want it there is no harm done; you are no use, that is all. If she *does* want it, and will not *take* it: there are ways—but the simple way is sincere, and will do. Ha; my grandfather used to say that no living man, prince or pauper, could refuse a five-pound note if you crackled it under his nose. Why did I not get a thousand-pound note and crackle it under your nose? Wouldn't you like to take it and burn it before my face? *Quel geste!* I could take the number, swear to the burning, get another one, and crackle that too. Stella, if those bankers—no: don't be angry; I only say *if, if, if, if.* And so enough of that. Only, dearest, if you ever want anything ever so little, remember, crackle, crackle, crackle, crackle.

[33]

CAMPBELL. Your letter! Well I never! I never did! Would you mind *lending* me some bacteria? The doctors can't find any in my blood and they want some to cook and replace. They say now a horse's, but I would much rather have yours. Oh! I long for you to be here and throw all three doctors out the window. If you don't come to see me soon, there won't be a "me" to see! Ask Charlotte to be kind. Even if she does think me a lunatic or an adventuress, she might let you call on me while I'm ill. That's perfectly respectable. And I can be terribly proper.

SHAW. No. It is best to ask her nothing; I barely mention your name. Yesterday Charlotte overheard our telephone conversation and the effect was dreadful; it hurts me miserably to see anyone suffer like that. I must, it seems, murder myself or else murder her. Well, I daresay, it is good for us all to suffer; but it is hard that the weak should suffer the most. I throw my desperate hands to heaven and ask why one cannot make one beloved woman happy without sacrificing another.

CAMPBELL. Oh darling, don't be silly. I had a dream about Charlotte last night. She shook hands with me warmly and smiled and said, "I thought you were a bird of paradise but you are only a silly goose." The dream ended with my jumping out of bed and taking a taxi to—you know where. Stella, *la dangereuse.* [*She takes her feet off footstool and addresses audience*] Then after that, I began to recover—I went into a nursing home where they pummeled me in the mornings and strapped me on a board at night; but by January I was able to move about and in February visitors were let come in to see me—and they came by the scores—all the people I knew in London and some I didn't. One came every day bringing roses and gaiety into my room. George Cornwallis-West. It wasn't long before Mr. Shaw noticed his visits and then he began to act very peculiarly indeed.

SHAW. Can it be true? My sprite tells me you are jilting me! Tell me, am I spurned indeed? Must I stop making verses? Though I confess I can think of no rhyme for "Stella" but "umbrella" and "too damn *well*" I love "Mrs. Camp*bell.*" Though I like George I say he is young and I am old. So let him wait until I am tired of you.

CAMPBELL. Be calm dearest Joey, be gentle with fools. Poor you. Awful as it is, it is nothing compared to the humiliation I feel with Charlotte while I am without a husband. Now I know there is nothing you can do about that, but there is a great deal George can do. So, please! Will you come to a nice little supper party of bananas and apples and nuts, and Charlotte, too, if she will stop regarding me as a middle-aged minx.

SHAW. Does Charlotte know something about George that I do not? She has suddenly metamorphosed from a monster into a green-eyed mermaid. Amazing, she actually refers to you now without fury. What is it?

CAMPBELL. Her woman's instinct my dear, and the gossip of how attractive George is, and how interested he is in me. But enough of that! I have just heard of the illness of your beloved mother. I remember you once said, "It is from her I derive my brains and character which does her credit." Oh Joey! I know how devotedly you love her. If she leaves us, it will be a great loss.

SHAW. Mamma, yes! She cut a wisdom tooth when she was eighty! and now it is the end, they say. The world is changing horribly . . . G.B.S.

He crosses dejectedly down and around stage-right side of desk so he ends the circle up-right, where he begins funeral speech.

CAMPBELL. I have just been told the sad news. May she rest in peace! I had a mother who loved only Dante, and whose soul was steeped in beauty. When you can, let me hear from you.

SHAW [*There is the minimum of movement in this*

speech. The middle section should be almost to him-
self as if he were still there in the crematorium. The
whole is filled with love *for his mother.* CAMPBELL
listens intently] 22nd February 1913. What a day! I
must write to you about it, because there is no one
else who didn't hate her mother, and even who doesn't
hate her children. Whether you are an Italian peasant
or a superwoman I cannot yet find out; but anyhow
your mother was not the Enemy. Why does a funeral
always sharpen one's sense of humor and rouse one's
spirits? This one was a complete success. No burial
horrors. No mourners in black, snivelling and wallow-
ing in induced grief. Nobody knew except myself,
Granville-Barker, and the undertaker. Since I could
not have a splendid procession with lovely colors and
flashing life and triumphant music, it was best with
us three. I particularly mention the undertaker because the humor of the occasion began with him. I
walked to the Crematorium with Barker; and there
came also the undertaker presently with his hearse,
which had walked conscientiously at a funeral pace
through the cold; though my mother would have pre-
ferred an invigorating trot. The undertaker approached
me in the character of a man shattered with grief; and
I, hard as nails and in loyally high spirits (rejoicing
irrepressibly in my mother's memory), tried to convey

to him that this professional chicanery, as I took it to be, was quite unnecessary. And lo! it wasn't professional chicanery at all. He had done all sorts of work for her for years, and was actualy and really in a state about losing her. And the coffin was covered with violet cloth—not black. I must rewrite that burial service; there are things in it that are deader than anyone it has ever been read over; still with all its drawbacks it is the most beautiful thing that can be read as yet. And the parson did not gabble it in the horrible manner common on such occasions. With Barker and myself for his congregation (and Mamma) he did it with his utmost feeling and sincerity. At the passage "earth to earth, ashes to ashes, dust to dust" there was a little alteration of the words to suit the process. A door opened in the wall: and the violet coffin mysteriously passed out through it and vanished as it closed. People think that door the door of the furnace; but it isn't. I went behind the scenes at the end of the service and saw the *real* thing. People are afraid to see it; but it is *wonderful*. I found there the violet coffin opposite another door, a real unmistakable furnace door this time; when it lifted there was a plain little chamber of cement and firebrick. No heat, no noise. No roaring draft. No flame. No fuel. It looked cool, clean, sunny. You would have walked in or put your hand in without misgiving. Then the violet coffin moved again and went in, feet first. And behold! The feet burst miraculously into streaming ribbons of garnet-colored lovely flame, smokeless and eager, like Pentecostal tongues, and as the whole coffin passed in it sprang into flame all over; and my mother became that beautiful fire. The door fell; and they said that if we wanted to see it all through, we should come back in an hour and a half. I remembered the wasted little figure with the wonderful face, and said "Too long" to myself; but off we went. When we returned, the end was wildly funny, Mamma would have enjoyed it enormously. We looked down through an opening in the floor. There we saw a roomy kitchen, with a big cement table and two cooks busy at it. They had little tongs in their hands, and they were deftly and busily picking nails and scraps of coffin handles out of Mamma's dainty little heap of ashes and samples of bone. Mamma herself being at that moment leaning over beside me, shaking with laughter. Then they swept her into a sieve, and shook her out: so that there was a heap of dust and a heap of bone scraps. And Mamma said in my ear, "Which of the two heaps is me, I wonder!" And that merry episode was the end, except for making dust of the bone scraps and scattering them on a flower bed. O grave, where is thy victory? And so good-night, friend, who understands about one's mother [*He turns directly to her*] and *other* things.

CAMPBELL. I have been thinking a great deal and lo, I find I *adore* sentiment—the sentiment of love, of youth, of religion, of babies, of nursery fires—and a thousand things—and I adore acrobats too, on wires— or mental, like you. Oh, dear—oh, dear—dear—dear —dear. All roads lead to the hole in the ground or the door in the oven. I'm stumped. [*She gets up and addresses audience*] Then quite suddenly the physicians who attended me—the two knights and the baronet— pronounced me well.

SHAW [*to audience*] And *Pygmalion* was announced at last for April 1914.

CAMPBELL. [*to audience*] I knew myself and my strength. I needed to go away for a bit to sort things out. I knew I was too old for Eliza and I had naturally heard—as who hadn't?—the rumors about Joey's behavior at rehearsals; how he bullied his actors mercilessly until he got what he wanted. And I knew I must be thoroughly prepared. But there was a personal reason, too, for me to be out of London just now; my "everyday visitor" George Cornwallis-West. I was beginning to feel a great "understanding" was growing between us and I knew a romance at this time was unwise, both for the play and for my relationship with

Joey. So, a few days by the sea, alone with my maid and my dog, were prescribed, and it was best to let Joey know about it as casually as possible. I had had a splinter pulled out from under my nail. He had held my hand. I used that as an excuse for my note. [*To Shaw*] Dear Joey, you were all kindness and sympathy yesterday and I am sure it would have hurt much more if you hadn't been there. Oh, by the way, I'm going down to Sandwich tomorrow for a few days. I want to be alone by the sea and I will hide in the sands somewhere until the play begins. How are strength and steadiness to come to me otherwise, and Eliza? But I must go alone.

SHAW. My dearest love, solitude is wonderful but not when you are alone! Are you very low in the reaction after the pain? If I were with you I would cheat that reaction somehow—hide you from it in my arms —say all sorts of things (all true) to make you forget it. Solitude! When I am solitary you are always with me. When you are solitary by the sea where shall I be? Shall I come?

CAMPBELL. What a dear letter. When you are tender like this a thousand cherubs peep out from your purple and black wings. It's getting difficult not to love you more than I ought to love you. Offend me quickly to pull me together again—but don't come here. By the sea I *must* be *alone!*

SHAW [*to audience*] But how could I stay in London now she was herself again? I packed my bag, caught the next train from Victoria and shortly after lunch I was running along the sands to her hotel, singing all the way. Stella was in the writing room scribbling notes. I tiptoed up behind her. [*To her*] Stella! Stella Stellarum!

CAMPBELL. Joey! What on earth are you doing here? [*Rising*] Didn't you read my letter? Please, will you go back to London at once. At *once*. Very well, if you won't go I will. One of us must behave like a gentleman! Joey, please! [*To audience*] But he wouldn't go. I saw him again that evening for dinner and at eleven o'clock, overcome with sleepiness, to get him back to his hotel, I agreed to go bathing first thing next morning. But it was only a ruse. When he arrived, bathing costume and all, we had already driven away, leaving a note with the chambermaid.

SHAW [*reading note*] "When you get this I will have gone. Good-by. I am still very tired. It was you who should have gone. You were more fit for a journey than I. Stella." [*He crumbles up the letter and turns to her*] Very well, go! The loss of a woman is not the end of the world. The sun shines; it is pleasant to swim; it is good to work; my soul can stand alone! But I am deeply, deeply, deeply wounded. Bah! You have no nerve, you have no brain. There is nothing really frank in our comradeship after all. You run after life furtively and when it turns and opens its arms to you you run away. Go then. The Shavian oxygen burns up your little lungs; seek some stuffiness that suits you. You have wounded my vanity. An inconceivable audacity; an unpardonable crime! You don't care! No you don't. It was I who cared, you never did! Not for George, neither. No, though you may think so. You won't marry George; at the last minute you will funk him or be ousted by a bolder soul. Even if *I* had been secretly bored to distraction I would have stayed on in fire rather than have dealt *you* the enormous blow of *deserting* you. But what do you know of such things? You! Why, you could tear the strings out of an archangel's harp to tie up parcels!

CAMPBELL. Stop. Stop. You vagabond, you blind man you. You weaver of words, you poor thing unable to understand a mere woman. You lost me because you never found me. I said I'd behave like a gentleman and I did. You in your broomstick and sheet! You smother me with your bellows of self and your egotistical snortings!

SHAW. But you promised! What did you want, oysters and champagne? Well, I've got something out of the trip anyway; I've written the play already. Act one: Stella says [*He imitates Stella*]: Let us bathe before breakfast at a quarter to eight and George Bernard Shaw says No, at eight! [*Imitating her*] too late! Make it quarter to eight! [*As himself*] Please, not before eight! Curtain to act one! Act Two: Joey comes to bathe. Smiling chambermaid comes out [*He imitates the maid's high voice*] They're gone, sir. [*As himself*] What? Today? Ha, ha. I thought it was tomorrow. [*In the maid's voice blatantly aside to the audience*] What a charming voice and smile that old sport has. *He* don't care! Curtain! He does care though. Useless these letters, the wound will not heal!

CAMPBELL. But don't you remember? When the waiter brought the ginger beer he said, "You have already paid your bill, so the ginger beer will be one shilling." I thought that you would have guessed then that I was going since I had paid the bill. But you were too sleepy. I owe you a shilling! Why do you go on scolding me for the woman I am and not the woman you would have me be. When I see you I can tell you what will make all clear. Do you think it was nothing to me to hurt my friend. Joey, dear, don't be hurt. Please, *please, please*.

SHAW. 31st December, 1913 . . .

CAMPBELL. In the New Year may you play with the

moon and kiss the stars—and the earth lie in your lap . . .

SHAW. New Year's Eve. O night of all nights in the year. Do you remember last New Year's Eve? I am actually asking you do you remember it? Was it anything to you except that you were ill? *I* remember it; it tears me all to pieces. I believe we were both well *then,* and have been ill ever since. For what is this senseless walking about, this business, this repainting and repapering, but disease and madness? On that last New Year's Eve and all the eves that went before it, there was Eternity and Beauty, infinite, boundless loveliness and content. I think of it with a tragic despair: for you have wakened the latent tragedy in me, broken through my proud overbearing gaiety that carried all the tragedies of the world like feathers and stuck them in my cap and laughed. And if your part in it was an illusion, then am I as lonely as God. Therefore you must still be the Mother of Angels to me, still from time to time put on your divinity and sit in the heavens with me. For that, with all our assumed cleverness, is all we two are really fit for. Remember this always for in this I am deeply faithful to you—faithful beyond all love. Be faithful to me in it and I will forgive you though you betray me in everything else—forgive you, bless you, honor you and adore you. *Super hanc Stellam* will

I build my Church. [*Moves toward her*] And now let us again hear the bells ring: you on your throne in your blue hood, and I watching and praying, not on my knees, but at my fullest stature. For you I wear my head nearest the skies.

He crosses near her chair during latter part of speech and puts out his hand on final line.

CAMPBELL [*she takes his hand*] Oh, Joey! If I could write letters like you, I would write letters to God.

They drop hands. He crosses to his desk. She picks up script of Pygmalion, *rises and thumbs through it.*

SHAW [*to audience*] Pygmalion begins at last. After all the talking and waiting we began rehearsals at His Majesty's Theatre in the middle of February, 1914, with Mrs. Patrick Campbell as Eliza and Sir Herbert Beerbohm Tree as Higgins. The battle lines were drawn and there was no turning back.

CAMPBELL [*to Shaw as she holds script*] Oh, goodness, we're in for it—and let's be *very* clever—I'll be tame as a mouse and oh, so obedient—I wonder if you'll get what you want out of me, I feel a little afraid.

SHAW [*to audience*] And indeed we all had reason to be apprehensive. Stella, at the age of forty-nine, was asked to play a girl still in her teens . . . and with a cockney accent, at that. And now, the heavy work started. [*He moves his chair stage center*] After the

[46]

first reading we began to rehearse it scene by scene. [*To Campbell*] Now, Stella, as you know, the play begins under the arches of St. Paul's Church in Covent Garden. As it is a drizzly London night, several persons are sheltering here—waiting for their cars after the evening's performance at the Opera. Among them, the celebrated professor, Henry Higgins, the world's foremost authority on phonetics. And, amid the general hubbub, we gradually become aware of your voice, Stella, as you approach, [*She begins to pantomime selling violets*] coming in out of the rain, a slovenly, bedraggled flower girl, Eliza Doolittle.

CAMPBELL (*as* ELIZA) Baw ya flah orf a por gal!

SHAW. Higgins springs to attention and whips out his pencil.

CAMPBELL (ELIZA) Voylets . . . voylets . . . who'll buy my voylets?

SHAW. You drop a bunch in the muddy street and seeing them ruined, cry . . .

CAMPBELL (ELIZA) [*she pantomimes dropping bunch and picking it up*] Ah—ah—aw—aw—oooo. . . .

SHAW. Higgins writes furiously, "What a sound!—what a delicious sound!"

CAMPBELL (ELIZA) 'Ere now! Whatcher tiken dawn . . . I'm a good gal, I am—I ain't done nuffink.

SHAW. No, no—Stella— Read it as if you are talking to a policeman, not a doctor—try it again.

BOTH. I ain't done nuffink.

SHAW. That's better.

CAMPBELL. I shall die over this accent, anyway. You wrote her a cockney just to torment me.

SHAW. Stella!

CAMPBELL. Oh, very well . . . (*as* ELIZA) 'Ere now. Whatcher takin' down—I'm a good gal, I am.

SHAW (*as* HIGGINS) Woman! Cease this detestable boohooing instantly or else seek shelter elsewhere.

CAMPBELL (ELIZA) I've a right to be here if I like, same as you.

She sits, whimpering and sniveling, on the chair he has placed for her.

SHAW (HIGGINS) [*he crosses around behind her on this speech*] A woman who utters such depressing and disgusting sounds has no right to be anywhere—no right to live. Remember that you are a human being with a soul and the divine gift of articulate speech; that your native language is the language of Milton and the Bible; and don't sit there crooning like a bilious pigeon.

CAMPBELL (ELIZA) Ah—ah—aw—aw—oooo . . .

SHAW (HIGGINS) You see this creature with her curbstone English! Well, sir, in six months, I could pass that girl off as a duchess at an ambassador's garden party.

CAMPBELL (ELIZA) What's that you say?

SHAW (HIGGINS) Yes, you squashed cabbage leaf, you incarnate insult to the English language. I could pass you off as the Queen of Sheba.

CAMPBELL (ELIZA) [*happily*] Ah—ah—aw—aw—oooo . .

SHAW. Well, now, that's not so hard, is it, Stella? We might begin to get it in a month or so— [*Crossing back to his desk*] I am amazed you find it so difficult to be common. Just be a little human—it might do instead!

CAMPBELL [*rises in place*] Well! You've already made me feel thoroughly uncomfortable and this is only the fourth day—you'd better let Charlotte know you are going to make silk purses out of a sow's ears. I'm sorry if I'm difficult . . . [*Crosses toward her desk. Stops and turns back*] But you must admit Eliza is a little more of a lady in the tea scene than you seem to allow.

SHAW. Exactly—what I have written is one-half a lady and one-half a slut, but you are trying to look a slut and play a lady. It simply won't work. And what is the reason for that new "turn away" that's been sneaking in lately?

CAMPBELL. Sneaking in? I like that! I've got to do

something. All that business you've given Tree simply won't hold up, that's all.

SHAW. And neither will your smile. Why do you think I gave him the apple in the first place?

CAMPBELL. Tree takes five minutes between each word and each bite of that apple! I have a facial paralysis from trying to express any sort of intelligent feeling. That's why I turn away. I'm simply hiding my face till it's well again. [*She turns and walks upstage*]

SHAW. Then that is why your face looks like a burst paper bag! [*He crosses away*]

CAMPBELL [*turning back*] Don't think you're hurting me—not at all—I've told you that I was an utter silly-billy in that scene. What you think of me and my poor talent, I am not concerned with now.

SHAW. The "at home" scene still worries me a little —I'll come over to your house in Kensington Square tonight and go over it with you—you still make it too much like a music-hall turn.

CAMPBELL [*folding up shawl*] You've written a music-hall turn—and you need all the laughs you can get in your play.

SHAW. Now, then—we'll start after you've arrived and sat down . . . [*He takes her chair and moves it into the center*] and remember to walk like a lady! The others are on each side of you—Mrs. Eynsford Hill here, Freddie there, Mrs. Higgins here. Mrs. Higgins says, "Will it rain, do you think?"

CAMPBELL (*as* ELIZA) [*enunciating*] The shallow depression in the west of these islands moves slowly in an easterly direction—there are no indications of any great change in the barometrical situation.

SHAW [*as* FREDDIE] Oh, I say! Ha! Ha!

CAMPBELL (ELIZA) [*looking daggers*] What are you sniggering about, young man? I bet I got it right.

SHAW (*as* MRS. HIGGINS) Yes. [*Pointing to indicate Mrs. Higgins' position*] I do hope it won't turn cold. There's so much influenza about.

CAMPBELL (ELIZA) My aunt died of influenza, so they said.

SHAW (MRS. HIGGINS) Really!

CAMPBELL (ELIZA) But it's my belief they done the old woman in.

SHAW (MRS. HIGGINS) Done her in!

CAMPBELL (ELIZA) Ye-e-s, Lord love you! Why should she die of influenza? She come through diphtheria right enough, the year before. Fairly blue with it, she was. They all thought she was dead. But my father, he kept ladling gin down her throat till she come to so sudden that she bit the bowl off the spoon. What call would a woman with that strength in her have to die of influenza? And what become of her new straw hat that should have come to me? Somebody pinched it; and what I say is, them as pinched it, done her in.

SHAW (*as* MRS. EYNSFORD HILL) You surely don't believe that your aunt was killed?

CAMPBELL (ELIZA) Do I not? Them she lived with, would have killed her for a hat-pin, let alone a hat.

SHAW (*as* MRS. HIGGINS) But it can't have been right for your father to pour spirits down her throat like that. It might have killed her.

CAMPBELL (ELIZA) Not her. Gin was mother's milk to her. Besides, he'd poured so much down his own throat, that he knew the good of it.

SHAW (MRS. HIGGINS) Good Heavens!

CAMPBELL (ELIZA) It never did him no harm, what I could see. But then he did not keep it up regular. On the burst as you might say.

SHAW. Cheerfully, Stella, cheerfully. "On the burst!"

BOTH [*they repeat it metronomically together with a rising tempo. He conducts*] On the burst, as you might say, from time to time. And always more agreeable when he had a drop in!

CAMPBELL (ELIZA) Well, I'm afraid I must be going. Good-by, Mrs. Higgins.

SHAW (*as* MRS. HIGGINS) Good-by.

CAMPBELL (ELIZA) Good-by, Mrs. Eynsford Hill.

SHAW (*as* MRS. EYNSFORD HILL) Good-by.

CAMPBELL (ELIZA) Good-by, all.

SHAW (*as* FREDDIE) If you are walking across the Park, Miss Doolittle, may I . . .

CAMPBELL (ELIZA) Walk! Not bloody likely! I'm going home in a taxi.

SHAW. By George, Stella, we've got it. You can be wonderful when you really try. Good-night!

He puts his chair back in place at end of this speech.

CAMPBELL. Joey, there's only four days to go. But I'm afraid it isn't *right* enough.

SHAW [*stooping up from replacing chair*] No, it's not. It's at the end of the play, that's where you still go off. You can boil a scene in bread and milk better than anyone I know, but this, beloved, would be better boiled in brandy. Perhaps it might help if you could imagine Higgins to be me, then you could be properly scornful. And remember to speak up. Sometimes at the back of the theater I can't hear a word you say.

CAMPBELL [*walks about like a nervous, caged animal*] Oh, you are a horrible man, I know my performance is a mere masquerade, but I've told you from the beginning that I'm years too old for the part and I can't do a cockney to "save me neck" *or* yours. But I can be heard in any theater in the world, no matter what may be the matter with your ears.

She turns angrily away.

SHAW. Don't give up. It's all there I tell you! But still without the shape of a performance; the despair, the human soul, the social problem: until you get them all together I'll never admit that you can play either Eliza or Shaw.

CAMPBELL [*still pacing*] I really do hope you'll make heaps of money, Joey, and keep your gay belief that only you and your play did it, and that without you there would have been but failure and fools. Any more directions you may have for me, give them through the stage manager.

She replaces her chair emphatically! She begins to walk away but is arrested by "tonight is the night."

SHAW. Final orders! Tonight is the night! A great deal will depend on whether you are inspired at the last moment. You are not, like me, a great general. I don't like fighting, I like conquering. But you think you like fighting and now you will have to succeed, sword in hand; and the wonderful thing, Stella, is that I know you will; succeed with dash and brilliancy and resolution.

CAMPBELL. I'll obey your orders faithfully, I am so thankful you carried through your giant's work to the finish.

SHAW. And so, *avanti!*

CAMPBELL [*to audience*] The play went like a dream, it was filled with heavenly laughter. Surely no first night in the world had ever gone so joyously.

SHAW [*to audience*] With each act the laughter and the applause became louder and more enthusiastic until by the end it was apparent that Stella had taken the whole of London by storm and we were both pitched overnight to the very top of the heap. A party had been arranged after the opening. But when I went to fetch Stella, I was in for a shock. Oh! she had a knack for dramatic timing. She was on the point of leaving the stage door.

CAMPBELL [*walks as if to leave stage. She is startled to see Shaw*] Joey . . .

SHAW [*facing her*] Aren't you going to the celebration? You're not going home . . . alone . . . tonight?

CAMPBELL. I'm not going alone. I'm going home with George. He's waiting for me in his motor car.

SHAW. George?

CAMPBELL. Yes. George Cornwallis-West. I married him last Wednesday.

Curtain

Act Two

Lights up. Enter CAMPBELL. *She speaks to audience as she walks.*

CAMPBELL. *Pygmalion* was the great success of the London season. But the year was 1914. A few months after our opening Belgium was invaded by Germany and all Europe was plunged into war. The theaters in London were closed. Both my husband and my son, Beo, had enlisted and were with the fighting forces at the front. I decided to take *Pygmalion* to America. Mr. Shaw, as usual so far ahead of the times as to be called traitor by much of the nation, was writing for the *New Statesman*.

SHAW [*entering; as if dictating, he walks to his desk*] We must lend our minds to the problem of how to redraw the map of Europe and reform its political constitutions so that this abominable and atrocious nuisance, a European war, shall not easily occur again.

CAMPBELL [*to audience*] Then his letters and Beo's letters began getting through to me in New York—before America was in the war.

She sits.

SHAW. Stella, this war is getting too silly for words. They make no headway and produce no result except kill, kill, kill. The Kaiser asks from time to time for another million men to be killed; and Kitchener asks for another million men to kill them. And now that they have settled the fact that their stupid fighting can't settle anything, and produces nothing but a perpetual Waterloo that nobody wins, why don't the women rise up and say, "We have the trouble of making these men; and if you don't stop killing them we shall refuse to make any more?" But alas, the women are just as idiotic as the men. And that is all, Stella. Might be a scrap of newspaper, might it not? Do you never ask yourself what has become of my sonnets?

He sits on stool.

CAMPBELL. No, I don't miss your sonnets!—or your love-making. I know you so well, Joey—just how much you appreciated me—and how little. I was out of pocket $7,750 getting the play across the country to San Francisco, in the sweltering heat and the one-night stands in the practically empty theaters. The people thought Bernard Shaw "highbrow stuff" and wouldn't come near you! They expressed great disappointment that we never spoke the title of the play; they wanted so much to know how it should be pronounced, whether Pyge-malion—or *Pig*-ma-lion! I have grown quite plain and my hair is getting gray, but then the newspapers in this country are enough to make us all maniacs. A few Sundays ago in enormous headlines "British Navy Sunk." I have been and am very anxious about my son Beo. He got ill in the trenches at the Dardanelles and was sent to Alexandria; only three men left out of his platoon. O the enormity and eternal bloody error of this war! I miss you very much; I wonder whether I will ever see you again. Stella.

SHAW. Dear Stella: I returned from Ireland with the survivors of the "Lusitania" through millions of submarines, all imaginary as it proved. I appeared on the London platform at the end of October and lectured twice on the war. Riots were expected; but the result was three hundred people turned away, and only two questions, both about Jesus Christ. Your photograph is too young and beautiful to be true; you should see *me*. I look seventy. The theater is passing away from me as a sort of wild oats; I go back to politics, religion and philosophy. They give me frightful headaches, but satisfy my soul.

CAMPBELL [*to audience*] After two long years in America, I returned in 1916 to London for George Alexander's revival of *Bella Donna*. My husband had escaped from Antwerp, but Beo had been sent back from the front. The war was getting more horrible every day—the casualty lists—the wounded in the streets! It was months before I heard from Joey again.

SHAW. Ayot St. Lawrence, Welwyn. 14th May 1916. Stella: I have had influenza, and in spite of a fortnight by the sea, I feel suicidal. My new volume should have been out a month ago, but there was no labor to print it, no labor to bind it, no ships to carry it to London, and no goods train taking less than three months to come to London from Edinburgh, where my printing is done. The sequel to *Pygmalion* is on page 191. It will not interest you; but George will read it. I assume that you are in London; but I don't care. I never felt so morose in my life. I can't write; nothing comes off but screeds for the papers, mostly about this blasted war. I am old and finished. I am creeping through a new play (to prevent myself crying) at odd moments, two or three speeches at a time. I don't know what it's about. I began it on the 4th March; and I have hardly come to the beginning of the first scene yet. This is a rotten world. George looked tired when he came back. I do not think he has long to live. You must be feeling very old and feeble. I wonder which is the easiest: charcoal, morphia, or prussic acid. Well, good-by: we shall probably never meet again. My address will soon be, The Crematorium, Golders Green, N.W. G.B.S.

CAMPBELL. Oh, dear me, as though I didn't know *all that* years ago! You poor, poor *rich* man. My beloved Beo is in great danger and my heart aches and the hours are heavy.

SHAW. Ayot St. Lawrence. 7th March 1917. You have sent me half a letter, scrawled in a most uneducated manner. Send me the rest and I will answer it. What I have seems to be the last two sheets. Let me have the first six. There are three depths of illiteracy, each deeper than the one before. (1) The illiteracy of those illiterate enough not to know that they are illiterate. (2) The illiteracy of Eliza, who couldn't even read the end of her own story. (3) The illiteracy of those who have never read my works. There is only one person alive who is such a monster of illiteracy as to combine these three illiteracies in her single brain. And I, the greatest living Master of Letters, made a Perfect Spectacle of myself with her before all Europe.

During the last part of Shaw's speech, CAMPBELL *has read a telegram which tells her her son is killed. She is lost in her grief as he finishes. She waits a moment.*

CAMPBELL. My beloved Beo is killed. You have seen

[61]

it in the papers. I feel he is asleep and will wake and come to me if I am quite strong and calm. Do you think Macdona would like me to play Eliza in the big towns with him? The chaplain writes that Beo and the Commanding Officer were standing at the top of the stairs of their dugout and a shell burst and killed them both instantaneously. I would like you to read the letter. It is full of tragic gentleness and praise of my brave son.

SHAW [*he tries to be kind: gives up*] It is no use. I cannot be sympathetic: these things simply make me furious. I want to swear. I *do* swear. Killed just because people are blasted fools. A chaplain, too, to say nice things about it. It is not his business to say nice things about it, but to shout that "the voice of thy son's blood crieth unto God from the ground." No: don't show me the letter. To hell with your chaplain and his tragic gentleness! The next shell will probably blow *him* to bits; and some other chaplain will write such a nice letter to *his* mother. Gratifying, isn't it? Consoling. It only needs a letter from the King to make me feel that the shell was a blessing in disguise. No use going on like this, Stella. Wait a week; and then I shall be very clever and broad-minded again, and have forgotten all about him. I shall be quite as nice as the chaplain. Oh damn, damn, damn, damn, damn, damn,

damn, *damn. Damn!* And oh, dear, dear dear, dear, dear. [*Looks full at her only now*] Dearest!

CAMPBELL [*to audience*] If Beo had survived only a short time longer the war would have been over!

SHAW [*to audience*] With the armistice came a changed world—not politically, of course, but socially and economically. The fashions of King Edward were gone. George V's era was one that began to leave Stella behind; slowly, of course, but with a steady erosion. And our relationship took a tragi-comic turn. We suddenly found ourselves quarrelling like blazes over what was to be done with all the letters we'd written to each other and, curiously, seem both to have kept!

He walks back to desk.

CAMPBELL. January 1921. Joey—I have had a letter from a publisher that I would very much like your opinion upon. It is in the form of a contract for my book and I am afraid of it. Please let me know when you will be in town. A friend writes from New York, most enthusiastically about *Heartbreak House*—it *would* be a little unkind of you to leave me out if it is done here. She says it plays ever so much better than it reads! I wonder?

SHAW. Belovedovedest. I can't put you into the cast of *Heartbreak House*. You have intimidated me far too completely. I had rather fight Carpentier, and the rest of the cast would go on strike at once. What *I* dare not face, nobody else with any sense is likely to take on.

CAMPBELL. I will never get over it. It's such a pity I can't cry.

SHAW. Yes: it is a pity you can't cry. Any actress could. Crocodile!

CAMPBELL. This book business worries me.

SHAW. What have you written? Your life, or mine, or both?

CAMPBELL. You know I can neither write nor spell —neither can I spin—nor act. My wedding of words is unmoral—and my only idea of notation is a hyphen.

SHAW. Stella: I have settled it! Your book is to be called *The Autobiography of an Enchantress*. I think you will get under way quite easily if, after chronicling *The Second Mrs. Tanqueray*, you draw a double bar and spend the rest of your story on stage lovers and such like beginning with Tree, whose evening suit you stroked with passionate embraces of your heavily made-up arms until the poor man was like a zebra, and ending with Gerald Du Maurier, whose outpourings of admiration on the stage you punctuated by such asides as, "Good God, to have to play a scene like this to a face like that!"

CAMPBELL. Dear Joey: Your pen makes you drunk— I hear Charlotte is distressed! I hope this isn't true.

You never told her I was a gentleman or that I was merely swan-singing? It is a pity I ever read these letters again and it's a pity they are so lovely. And I am *glad* I never destroyed them. A copy is being made of the ones that I propose publishing—if you agree.

SHAW. Listen: You say that you will behave like a perfect gentleman. Well, a gentleman does not kiss and tell; so that settles that.

CAMPBELL. It is quite easy for me to come down from the clouds and realize there are other points of view than my own. I did indeed hate speaking of George to you. What I wanted was your clever opinion how to get just enough truth on the printed page. I thought you knew he left me two years ago.

SHAW. I am writing some autobiographical sketches for the proposed collected edition of my work. Suppose I put in *your* most intimate letters! Would any plea that I had your leave to do it save me from being put down as an inconceivable cad and coxcomb!

CAMPBELL. Joey—I am going to take you seriously; you say, "Suppose I put in *your* most intimate letters!" You may publish any letters of mine if you will correct the grammar and see to the punctuation.

SHAW. 'Round about 1895 or so, I wrote a wonderful string of love letters to Ellen Terry, and got a wonderful string of replies from her—and—

CAMPBELL. Why not get Ellen Terry to let me publish her love letters from you, *with* mine?

SHAW. I quite understand your intense reluctance to let me see the whole book. You are quite right! I shall ruthlessly tear it to pieces.

CAMPBELL. I long for you to see the whole book and to damn it—only not please at Ayot or 10 Adelphi Terrace. It would not take more than two hours to read. I would come up to London. Shall I?

SHAW. I warn you I shall have to connect your tidbits into dignified paragraphs, and, where I happen to know the truth, to substitute it for your "dramatization."

CAMPBELL. That's a silly word, "dramatization." I have done my best to be truthful and nontheatrical. You know I cannot write paragraphs—or those glorious long sentences of yours where, when I have arrived at the full stop I have to begin all over again to get my brain's balance!

SHAW. Why, there is one passage on which your George could get a divorce.

CAMPBELL. Let me know that passage.

SHAW. The cruelty of your making me read it!

CAMPBELL. Please, Joey, don't put on your suburban cap. You first said "I leave the publication, etc., to Mrs. Campbell's judgment."

SHAW. It takes a sledge hammer to knock anything into you that will make you see yourself as others *will* see you.

CAMPBELL. Say as many unkind and cruel things as you like—hit me with a thousand hammers—nobody can hurt me any more: is that not wonderful? Why do you object to the funny silliness of the world a hundred years from now. They will say I was your mistress and Granville-Barker our son!

SHAW. Now God defend me from idiots! I might just as well write essays on relativity to a female kingfisher. Very well! *Send* me your proofs. I will then tell you, brutally and dogmatically, what you may say and what you may not.

CAMPBELL. I wonder how you would have liked to send Shakespeare your first manuscript for him to damn, and his wife, and typist perhaps, to criticize, when he *could* have talked it over with you. I am afraid I am a little grumpy but perhaps if you had *never* made love to me I wouldn't mind your disagreeableness now —so please. As to "relativity," it is a philosophy that "empties the baby out with the bath water"—that's what you'll do with my book.

SHAW [*he comes near her and speaks with infinite patience as if to a child*] I must talk to you as a child of nine; you start from the position that the publication of intimate letters is not permissible among persons of honor. If they are love letters the difficulty is decupled, centupled, miltupled. If they are love letters from a married man to a woman who is not his wife, and who is engaged at the time to another man whom she has subsequently married, the difficulty becomes a wild impossibility. If the man publishes them he is a black-guard; if the woman publishes them, she is a rotter. [*He retreats furiously behind desk*] In the face of this you keep asking me why you should *not* publish the letters. You might as well ask me why you should not pick pockets or sell yourself on the street.

He turns his back and sulks.

CAMPBELL. I have been trying to get out of the letters with Hutchinson. You see! As soon as I saw your attitude was changing I behaved like a gentleman. Tell Charlotte not to worry. If necessary I will go to America and pay damages!

SHAW. It is no use bothering you with instructions. I have already done it. Nobody can reproach you now for publishing it as I have left it; and there is the requisite touch to set Charlotte right. It will be hard enough on her as it is to see her husband as the supreme ass of a drama of which you are the heroine.

CAMPBELL. I burn so with blushes at your confounded impudence, that I don't feel the cold. You have spoilt my book. You have spoilt my story. You have hidden from the world the one thing that would have done it good: lustless lions at play. May you freeze in that sea of ice in Dante's Inferno—I don't care. "Stolen your fig-leaf" indeed! You wear no fig-leaf in your letters.

SHAW [*over his shoulder to her*] Well then. Haven't you a letter from Pinero or any other of your authors? They will be furious if you leave them out; that is, if they have written any nice ones. You *must* have some more love letters. You cannot appear as a famous beauty who had only one catch; an old idiot of fifty-six. Will there be nobody to keep me in countenance?

CAMPBELL. You wait until you read Pinero's letters, Maeterlinck's, Barrie's, Edmund Gosse's, Burne-Jones', etc., etc.—you will be *sincerely* sorry you were second best. It is really sad: you creep on the ground, instead of flying in the air—through taking away those delicious letters. Publishers—money—rot! Ugh—

SHAW. Stella, you are such a fool! Such a—such a—such a fool! Do you know why I took away those "delicious letters" as you call them? Because I absolutely refuse any longer to play the horse to your Lady Godiva.

He crosses and sits on chair, arms folded.

CAMPBELL. It is just this epileptic revulsion that

keeps you from being the "superman" you would be—
and that you think you are. As the letters are now, they
are twaddle. As you sent them back to me they misrep-
resented both me and my feelings. I flirted with no
"super-philanderer." That is all lies. I was attached to
what has turned out a very ordinary individual—a
man who cannot realize that what he considers his
folly is really his honor. Only the sweep knows *all* that
is up the chimney. So then there is nothing left for me
to do but to hit you back with the poker, holding it
with both my hands—having no respect for your few
remaining transparent hairs—and to hit you flat dead.
I am going to publish exactly what I like—if you didn't
mean what you wrote, you shouldn't have written it.
Be thankful if I cut enough out, and leave enough in,
so that you dare face the public again. Start saying your
prayers. I have your letter giving me absolute permission. So you be civil. It's no use being a gentleman with
you—you've revoked, that's your game always. It's a
dreadful thing to have a vaulting mind that o'er leaps
itself and goes "potty"—that's what has happened to
you. I read in a paper yesterday, that you had ceased to
be popular. Had I had my way in the beginning, you
would have been as popular as Lord Byron, and Joseph!
Next time you try and fascinate an actress, don't use
her as a means of teasing Charlotte—*that* was the

ugliest thing you did. You don't amuse me: "We are not amused." A man who revokes is . . . well . . . an *Irishman*. [*To audience*] The book came out with some of the letters in it, much cut up of course, but still "something like" and the press was wonderful. Everyone said I'd shown the world the real Shaw, the human Shaw. And what a success he was having—his plays were all over the place—*Misalliance*, and *Getting Married*, and *Heartbreak House*, and finally, of course, *Saint Joan*. It was the day after that opened so triumphantly in London that I heard from him again —after nearly sixteen months of angry silence.

SHAW [*he stares stonily out front for a moment before saying*] Then you still live! [*He looks at her; rises, crosses up to his desk*] I went to Lyall Swete's dressing-room to give him a final word before the curtain rose; and he began to rave about you as the greatest actress in the world, swearing that you are as beautiful as ever, and that you had trained a perfect company to support you in perfect performances of Hedda and other plays. The man must be crazy. So now I forgive you the letters because there is a star somewhere on which you were right about them: and on that star we two should have been born. It was funny how few people knew. Well, are you quite well? And are you making plenty of money? And has your virgin loveliness really come back? And do you remember Tristan and Isolde and forget all our stupid conflicts? And did the book get you out of debt? And—and—and—what sort of life are you having generally? I shall be sixty-eight in July: that is about all *my* news, except what you may read in the papers.

CAMPBELL. Dear, dear Joey: Your letter at the theater gave me strange pleasure. Yes, the book brought in about £2,500. Will you take me to a matinee of *Saint Joan* this week? That would make up for a great deal. I have read your praises with so much pleasure—dear Joey—that you go deep, deep down into the human heart; that it is far the finest thing that you have ever done; and you are compared with Mr. Shakespeare, of course, and in one paper all they said was the youth of you. Sixty-eight indeed? Twenty-two—and I your grandmother. I never forget Tristan and Isolde—and you twenty-one and I seventeen—harps in the air.

SHAW. O Lord, Stella, it mustn't happen again until we are both dead. Then we can be added to Heloise and Abelard and all the rest of them. God intended you to play the serpent in Methuselah: I wrote it for your voice. When I told Edith Evans that she would have to enter bald-headed, old, half naked, and in rags, in a bevy of youths and maidens made as pretty as the stage could make them, and that in that ghastly condition she would out-fascinate them and play them clean out of existence, she believed, and did it. Sybil Thorndike for a whole month never let me doubt for a second that she regarded me as far superior to the Holy Trinity as a producer. And now Siddons and Rachel were never so praised and exalted as these twain. If you had only had faith as much as a grain of mustard seed.

CAMPBELL. You know I feel rather like the little black girl who, after the Englishman kissed her, ran to her mother and said "Englishman eatee me upee," and the next day crept back to the Englishman and said, "Eatee me upee some more."

SHAW [to audience] Stella began to fall on bad days —for a short time just before the great Depression, she was reduced to giving lectures on "Diction in Dramatic Art"—and her international reputation as a hellion had far outstripped the facts. But it was harder and harder for her to get new plays—her age was against her, for one thing, and her terms were always high— and her pride higher still.

CAMPBELL. February 1929. Dear Joey: I was under the impression that the great battle of life was fought in our youth—not a bit of it—it's when we are old, and our work not wanted, that it rages and goes on . . . and on . . . and on . . . My landlord won't al-

low pupils here, and to take a place to teach in—
well, it's too much of a venture. Anyway, it might not
be necessary if this play I have just been engaged to
open in—the part is an old Jewess of seventy with an
Austrian-French-Yiddish accent—is a success. I wonder if you will come and read *your* new play to me
as you have half promised you would.

SHAW. I can't read plays to a starving woman, Stella.
I hope the Jewess is a success, but I wish I'd had the
writing of her. Oh, what are we to do about you?
What about a benefit? Sybil Thorndike says that there
are plenty of artists, who like herself, adored you and
would do anything for you. They never played with
you, you demon! Ellen Terry had a benefit that en-
abled her to retire and die in comfort.

CAMPBELL. I'm not starving, I eat more than you do.
And I don't want a benefit. I sent a check for £25 to
Ellen Terry's which she acknowledged with a letter
beginning: "Dear Sir." The Jewess—the play is called
The Matriarch, you will have seen it in the press. The
Jewess will disgrace me if I make a success of her and
I'll never get another engagement if I don't. Joey dear,
please, please, please—you who once wrote that you
were my "friend world without end"—come and read
your play to me. We open next week and after that
you can come—Thursday, Friday, I am free until 4:30,

or Saturday. I am dying to know what it's about.

SHAW. I went yesterday to see *The Matriarch* and the critics are right about you for once—you have staged a sensational comeback; bravo Stella! And it is all yours and nobody else's—and that wicked caricature of you in *Punch* is good for business. But oh, my lady of sorrows, *what* a play! Two hours of artless, vindictive realism about this horribly clever sheeny woman in which *you* have to keep the audience from rushing out of the house and down a steep place into the sea! The audience is held only by the fact that Mrs. Patrick Campbell is jabbering and by the hopes that presently a bit of drama might come her way at last. There is that one good scene with you in the clever red dress but oh, if G. B. Stern (G.B.S., Junior, I notice) had only known her business! Tell GBS Junior to see my new play and see what a gorgeous success you are when *I* write your parts. You have saved her from being stoned! GBS Senior. As to the *Apple Cart*, the honest truth is that I am too shy to read you the only scene in that play that would interest you.

CAMPBELL [*rises*] What's this! I went to the Selfridge Ball last night and met Miss Edith Evans, who gazed eagerly at me, saying she was playing me in the *Apple Cart*. Everyone was talking of nothing else. The infamy of it—and that I must write to you at once—

that it is a national calamity, an insult—etc., etc.

She paces.

SHAW [*interrupting*] Now you must not talk too much. There is of course nothing that could give any clue to the public—above all to the press. It can be a secret between us.

CAMPBELL. How can it be a "secret" between us— when Edith Evans told me she was playing *me?*

SHAW. Edith Evans guessed of course. Perhaps half a dozen others know or think they know! For only you and I will ever know. But the press must never get hold of it.

CAMPBELL. No, Joey. If I had the script here I would talk it over with my lawyer—I am sure, in its suggestiveness, it is libelous and ought not to be presented.

SHAW. I don't feel it to be a bit wrong. It plays magnificently.

CAMPBELL. Oh! You *are* mountebank.

She crosses to window and glares out.

SHAW. Of course! We are a pair of mountebanks; but why, oh, why do you get nothing out of me, though I get everything out of you? Mrs. Hesione Hushabye in *Heartbreak House,* the Serpent in *Methuselah,* whom I always hear speaking with your voice, and Orinthia: all you, to say nothing of Eliza, who was only a joke. You are the vamp and I the victim; yet it is I who suck your blood and fatten on it whilst you lose everything! But I am as right about this play as you were about the letters—you will see. "My Dearest Liar" is there for all the world to love as I did. The scene is a reminiscence of our afternoons in Kensington Square in the old days. Now then, you might be surprised at its purity after all the fuss. I will come to your house tonight and we will read the scene aloud, together. [*Crosses to Stella with script*] Here is the script. [*She takes it grudgingly*] "Orinthia," you are. The scene is in Orinthia's boudoir. [*He moves her chair out to center*] You are at the writing table scribbling notes. Romantically beautiful and beautifully dressed. As the table is against the wall, your back alone is visible. King Magnus enters and waits on the threshold— you say . . .

CAMPBELL (*as* ORINTHIA) Who is that?
She sits to read

SHAW (*as* MAGNUS) His Majesty, the King.

CAMPBELL (ORINTHIA) Tell the King I don't want to see him.

SHAW (MAGNUS) He awaits your pleasure—He comes down and sits.

He brings his chair over and places it near her. Stage left.

CAMPBELL (ORINTHIA) Go away—A pause—I won't

speak to you—Another pause—If my private rooms
are to be broken into at any moment because they
are in the Palace and the King is not a gentleman, I
must take a house outside.

SHAW (MAGNUS) What is our quarrel today, beloved?

CAMPBELL (ORINTHIA) Ask your conscience.

SHAW (MAGNUS) I have none when you are concerned. You must tell me.

CAMPBELL (ORINTHIA) There, look at this book.
(She shows him the book.)

SHAW (MAGNUS) What is this?

CAMPBELL (ORINTHIA) Read the first three words—
if you dare.

SHAW (MAGNUS) "Orinthia, my beloved."

CAMPBELL (ORINTHIA) The name you pretended to
invent especially for me. You are the King of Liars
and Humbugs. (As CAMPBELL) That's very true, Joey.

SHAW. Just read the lines, Stella.

CAMPBELL (as ORINTHIA) She turns away.

SHAW. You needn't read the directions, Stella! (As
MAGNUS) And don't pretend to be hurt unless you
really are, dearest. It wrings my heart.

CAMPBELL (ORINTHIA) Since when have you set up
a heart? Did you buy that too, secondhand? (As
CAMPBELL) I like that. (As ORINTHIA) Listen to me,

Magnus. Why can you not be a real king?

SHAW (MAGNUS) In what way, belovedest?

CAMPBELL (ORINTHIA) What you need to make you a real king is a real queen.

SHAW (MAGNUS) But I have got one.

CAMPBELL (ORINTHIA) Oh, you are blind. You are worse than blind: you have low tastes. Heaven is offering you a rose; and you cling to a cabbage. (As CAMPBELL) Is that nice to Charlotte, Joey?

SHAW. It's a very apt metaphor, beloved. But what wise man if you force him to choose between doing without roses and doing without cabbages, would not secure the cabbages? Besides, you should know better than anyone else that when a man gets tired of his wife and leaves her it is never because she has lost her good looks. The new love is often older and uglier than the old.

CAMPBELL. Why should I know it better than anyone else?

SHAW. Why, because you have been married twice; and both your husbands have run away from you to much plainer and stupider women.

CAMPBELL. Shall I tell you why these men could not live with me? It was because I was higher than they were, and greater; they could not stand the strain of trying to live up to me.

SHAW. Good lord! It must be magnificent to have the consciousness of a goddess without ever doing anything to justify it.

CAMPBELL. All of this is ridiculous, Joey! *Pat* never left me. He died, *gloriously,* in the Boer War.

SHAW. Dearest Stella. Orinthia's husbands are not Pat or George. They are simply suggested by all the millions of men, who bit off more than they could chew.

CAMPBELL. *Rot!* This scene should never have been written.

She throws down script. He hands it back.

SHAW. Please go on reading, Stella.

CAMPBELL (*as* ORINTHIA) Magnus: when *are* you going to face my destiny, and your own?

SHAW (*as* MAGNUS) But my wife? The Queen? What is to become of my poor dear Jemima?

CAMPBELL (ORINTHIA) Oh, drown her: shoot her; tell your chauffeur to drive her into the Serpentine and leave her there. The woman makes you ridiculous.

SHAW (MAGNUS) I don't think I should like that. And the public would think it ill-natured.

CAMPBELL (ORINTHIA) Oh, you know what I mean. Divorce her. Make her divorce you. It is quite easy. Everyone does it when they need a change.

SHAW (MAGNUS) But I can't imagine what I should

do without Jemima.

CAMPBELL (ORINTHIA) Nobody else can imagine what you do with her. (*As* CAMPBELL) Really, Joey! (*As* ORINTHIA) You can see as much of Jemima as you like when we are married.

SHAW (MAGNUS) That is very magnanimous of you, my dear Orinthia, but I had rather marry the devil. Being a wife is not your job.

CAMPBELL (ORINTHIA) You think so because you have no imagination. I should make you more happy than any man has ever yet been on earth.

SHAW (MAGNUS) I defy you to make me more happy than our strangely innocent relations have already made me.

CAMPBELL. All this is preposterous!

She throws script down.

SHAW. There's only a bit more. Listen. [*He proceeds to read the rest*] Magnus says, looking at his watch, "Now I must go back to my work," and Orinthia says, "What work have you that is more important than being with me?"

"None."

"Then sit down."

"Yes," he says. "But tea is at half-past four."

Detaining him, she says, "Never mind your tea."

"You are only trying to make me late to annoy my

wife." He tries to rise but she pulls him back. "Let me go, please."

Orinthia holds on. "Why are you so afraid of your wife, you poor henpecked darling?"

"Henpecked! What do you call this? At least my wife does not restrain me by bodily violence." He tries to rise but she pulls him back. "Must I call the guard?"

"Do, do. It will be in all the papers tomorrow."

"Fiend, Orinthia! I command you!"

Orinthia laughs wildly, "Ha—ha—ha."

"Very well, you she-devil, you shall let go."

He tackles her in earnest. She flings her arms around him and holds on with mischievous enjoyment, finally dragging him to the floor, where they roll over one another. Suddenly the door is flung open and Sempronius, the first secretary, enters and gazes horror struck at the scandalous scene as the curtain falls.

SHAW [to CAMPBELL, *who is sitting in awe-struck horror*] There . . . have I not made a superb picture of you?

CAMPBELL. A gentleman does not kiss and tell, does he? Tear it up!

SHAW. What?

CAMPBELL. Tear it up and rewrite it with every scrap of that suburban back chat against Charlotte omitted. People will only say that old age and your superhuman vanity have robbed you of your common sense.

SHAW. You dare give yourself airs with me! Why, you out-Orinthia Orinthia.

CAMPBELL. I do, do I? Do you know what you are? You are what the Greeks called an amphisbaena.

SHAW. And what is that?

CAMPBELL. A creature, my dear Joey, with a head at each end of his body both walking in different directions!

She exits.

SHAW [*to audience*] Then seven years passed—years in which we both got older and more cantankerous—and farther apart than ever. [*He replaces his chair*] Stella had often been asked to go to Hollywood during the silent-picture era. She had always refused. But with the advent of the talkies, she thought she might have a try at it. And off she went—bag, baggage, and Pekingese. Though she had been in America many times and though she knew the country pretty well, she was completely unprepared for the life she found in Southern California. The kings and queens of Hollywood, though stars to all the world, were only celluloid names to her. And when she would meet them at the great parties in Beverly Hills, she simply couldn't resist a jibe. When she met Joan Crawford, she asked her "what she did." She said to John Gilbert, the greatest lover of the silent films, "Young man, you should try to get in the movies." On the set she behaved worse than ever. There is the story of her first film—she appeared on the lot and reported to the director—he said, "How do you do?" She said, "Well enough— could you tell me what it's all about and we'll get on with it?" "All right," he said, his hackles already up to the moon: "You're the widow of a seafaring man— only you don't know it yet—you're still waiting for him to come back. Now in this scene we'll take first, you come into the room, shut the door behind you, cross to the table, pick up a telescope, walk to the window, lift it up, raise the telescope to your eye and gaze steadily out to sea. Do you think you can do that?" She said she thought she could. "Very well, then, we'll shoot it—" and he rolled the cameras. Stella came into the room, closed the door behind her, crossed, picked up the telescope, went to the window, lifted it up, raised the telescope—turned to the director and said: "Which eye?" Needless to say, she wasn't too popular. Her parts got smaller and smaller and her money ran out. Oh, people tried to help her but it was no use. Alexander Woollcott said she was like a sinking ship firing upon her rescuers. Then, too, she had with her, her latest Pekingese, Moonbeam, and many were the things she refused to do because of him. She wouldn't come back to England because of the strict quarantine laws for dogs—and she wouldn't travel anywhere Moonbeam couldn't go. Finally, I suggested her for a small part in the Theatre Guild production of my new play, *The Millionairess*. But she thought they insulted her and she never went to see them. [*He replaces her chair by her desk*] In April 1935, after she'd heard about *The Millionairess* and thinking, [*He walks back toward his desk*] I'm afraid, that she'd been offered the leading part in it, she wrote from Hollywood.

He goes back to high stool and sits.

CAMPBELL [*enters upstage center. She gives the address as she slowly walks down and sits*] Sunset Tower, Sunset Boulevard. Hollywood, California. Dear Joey: It was very cheering, and very happy to get your letter. The Theatre Guild with their "subscription list" are a little intolerable; they treat artists like bales of cotton! I enclose my photograph taken six months ago—you will see I still hold together, should you really want me for your *Millionairess*—wouldn't that be wonderful? I wonder what she is like? What sort of things she says and does. Hollywood and the camera have taught me humility—deep humility: nobody need be afraid of me anymore. Three weeks' work in sixteen months— think of that misery—it has almost broken me up.

The studios say I am too celebrated for small parts, and too English to "star"—that Kalamazoo, Butte, Montana, and Seattle would not understand my English style and speech. Whenever I ring up my agents they answer: "M.G.M. is thinking of you but nothing suitable has come along." In retirement in Florence I could get along—but the urge won't be silenced . . . yet! It's odd that I don't mind brazenly cadging from you—I am in a very nasty jam—I can go on for six weeks perhaps, but it will be six weeks, perhaps more, before my allowance comes again, and then it won't be enough to put me straight. Will you help me? I don't mind being in the battle to the finish, but in this place one gets left in mid-air. Give a glance at Moonbeam's picture—could you have shut him up for six months? I wish you would visit one of those Quarantine homes. These poor little pet creatures have to suffer this torture through November fogs, and dark cold winter days—no voice they love to call their name —think what that means to a dog. For four hours on a stretch I watched so that the cruelty of it would sink into my bones—then I found it quite easy to put my dog before my country and my career! To him I am a goddess; how could I betray him? Do dear Joey take care of yourself and laze a little. As always, Stella.

SHAW. 11th August 1937. My antiquity, now extreme

at eighty-one, has obliged me to make a clearance among my papers and take measures generally for my probably imminent decease. I find that I have done a very wicked thing: I have kept all your letters in spite of my rule never to keep anything but necessary business memoranda. I kept Ellen Terry's because her handwriting made pictures of them which I could not burn; it would have been like burning a fifteenth-century French Book of Hours. I have no such excuse in your case. [*He rises*] I intended to buy from one of the fashionable locksmiths a beautiful jewel box big enough to hold the correspondence. But the only safe and easy plan is—just to stuff the letters into a vulgar set of registered envelopes and post them back to you so that you may have the complete correspondence in your hands. This will add to its value if you have to sell it. [*He crosses down, an old man, to the chair*] I rejoice to learn from the things you said to Agate that you ought not to have said, that you are still Stella. I wish I were still Joey; but I have to be content now to play Pantaloon.

He sits.

CAMPBELL [*during this speech the lights are dimmed, slightly, on Shaw*] New York. August 1937. Dearest Joey: I expect the registered envelopes will soon be here. Oh, dear me! There's a clutch at my heart—the desire to feel a child again will tempt me to read them. I don't understand why your ashes and Charlotte's ashes have to be scattered over the ground before your letters to me may be published. In fifty years' time life will be lived in the *air*. Nobody will read books—only those on gas and engines and screws and such things. But your letters to me will be carried in the airman's luggage because of the thrush in your throat! How it sings in your letters to me. That song will cease if those letters wait fifty years to be published. Eighty-one indeed! Remember the age of the song of the thrush—eighty-one thousand years or more! James Barrie's going makes one pause and so many others—speeding on. B's £500 a year provides for me. I live simply in the cheapest hotel in New York—$83 a month—and a refrigerator! I send you a profile of Moonbeam to melt your bosom. I send you also a chapter of my new book. If you read this you will understand my running away from Hollywood up into the mountains 7,000 feet above the sea and living there for seven months in a log cabin—wonderful months—indescribable beauty. I wrote at my book all day and half the night. Then alas! blood pressure and fainting fits started. The doctor's diagnosis was "working too hard in too high an altitude." The dear Irish housemaid used to come in on tiptoe every morning and say in a cheerful voice as I opened my eyes: "Sure and I thought it was dead you were, and there you are smiling and Moonbeam wagging his tail." Once she whispered: "I have some of my wages saved—if it is hard up you are, and not too proud to be taking from me." I told her to stop her talk—a dear, generous warm-hearted creature if ever there was one. Then I came back to New York and crept into this little hotel. I stayed in bed for nearly nine weeks—John Gielgud found me there and brought me flowers with tears in his eyes. He took me for a drive in the Park—gave me his arm and I walked slowly—and Moonbeam ran about. He asked me to come and see his Hamlet and criticize. I did. Now I am quite, *quite* well. I have just returned from playing in two summer theaters—Cohasset and Connecticut. An ovation and a cry for a speech each night were comforting so far as these things go. I don't expect you to answer this letter—I wanted you to know what I had been doing with life these last few years. It is your affection for me that will raise me a little out of the rut and place me somewhere near your side. I am proud and happy that it is so.

SHAW. Before I could answer this touching letter I fell gravely ill—some newspapers in America even announced my death—complete with obituaries and editorial sighs of relief. But as it turned out they were rather premature.

CAMPBELL. Lago di Garda, May 1938. Dear Joey: It is miserable to read of your illness in the newspapers. My beloved Italy has done wonders for me—I was carried on the boat when I left the States, and off the boat when I arrived at Boulogne—a rheumatic knee—four months of agony, and the American doctor had said, "eighteen months and crutches." When the Italian doctor saw it, he smiled and said: "I will have you dancing in a fortnight." And sure enough, twelve radium-mud packs for twelve days—has completely cured me. But the only thing that matters now is that you should get better—it troubles me very much.

SHAW [*he rises*] This is an age of miracles! [*Crosses back to desk*] I am back at my desk! The doctors seemed to have cured me at last by stabbing me in the seat once a fortnight with a monstrous hypodermic syringe. So for the moment I am not dead, though keeping me alive is pure officiousness, as I am eighty-two, and look it. [*Sits on stool*] Anyway that fellow Hitler will kill us all if the doctors don't.

CAMPBELL. Dear Joey: Do cease your comic allusions to age or you'll be missing the glory of the sunset. I've just heard of the huge success of your cinema *Pygmalion*—you must be making more money than you know what to do with. I wonder if you remember all the trouble I took—when was it? Nearly thirty years ago! How I took the play to Tree and begged him to ask you to come and read it to him—and said I would play Eliza. How we all stood your insults at rehearsals! How you nearly killed Tree with that sickly suburban pun, "I say Tree, must you be so Tree-acly." Of course you have forgotten everything or you would have sent a Christmas box. And you have dared to go about the world saying that *I* am impossible in the theater—because of that one day I couldn't stand it one more minute. [*Rises and advances to front of stage; points into audience*] I stood up and advanced to the footlights and said, "If Mr. Shaw doesn't leave the theater, I will!" And you dare accuse me of humiliating people! Since you first dipped your pen in the ink pot, what have you *ever* done?

She returns and sits.

SHAW. If only I had time to write your reminiscences for you I'd make you the most famous woman in Europe and America. I haven't any money and I have huge sums to pay the government next month; the cinema *Pygmalion* has not sent a penny my way yet. As to bringing you over, I had as soon bring the devil over. You would upset me and everybody else. You don't know how I have blessed that wretched little dog. If only you could write a true book entitled *Why, Though I Was a Wonderful Actress, No Manager Would Ever Engage Me Twice If He Could Possibly Help It*. But you couldn't—you never would.

CAMPBELL. *Preposterous. Six* engagements with Alexander—*nine* engagements with Forbes-Robertson—*four* with Gerald Du Maurier—*two* with Hare—*four* with Tree. But what's the use of bothering about your willful nonsense. If war comes what will happen to the letters, I wonder? I've stuffed them all into an old battered hatbox and I hide them under the bed at night. So there you are at last, Joey, *under* my bed. I am in one little room here, but I have an open wood fire—and a lovely view over the Tuileries Gardens—and the Parisian sun all day. The covered colonnades go all down the street so I can go out, wet or fine. The Duke and Duchess of Windsor live three doors down on my right. He looks tranquil—she looks calm. I see you have another play! At your age!

SHAW. Yes, my new play *Geneva* is horrible! The politest critic describes me as a dignified monkey shying coconuts at the audience. I went to see it the other day and it made me quite ill. Splendid for the actors though. The performances are like election meetings. I must stop making myself unpleasant. But I have to write plays like *Geneva*. It is not that I want to. It can't be helped—the war coming and all. "Joey" was the cleverest thing you ever invented—by far, by far, by far.

CAMPBELL. I have invented Joey? Your written words inspired me. If they were false, then Joey is an impostor. But there! I am not going to waste your time with any more of my "ridiculous" letters. We will meet in heaven; you will bow, I will curtsy, and the angels will say to each other: "They did not snatch at joy and spoil the winged world."

SHAW [*To audience. An old man again*] I was to hear from Stella only once more—then I wrote to her again, a month later. And that was all. Her letter was dated June 28, 1939. Hitler was massing his tanks before the Maginot Line and the Second World War was nearly upon us. I'd already sent word to Stella that they were considering her for a role in the film of my *Major Barbara*, but I wondered if she was still seriously in the field.

CAMPBELL. Yes: I am still seriously "in the field": but not, you know, as cannon fodder. A week or two ago I thought I would be heroic—I offered myself to the English Theatre here at £25 a week, or less. In answer they sent me a play to read: my part a Jewish mother with an idiot son whose weakness was to kill little girls and hide them in his mother's rag bag. My dialogue consisting of: "Oi, oi, oi; we shouldn't have left him alone." I asked the manager what made him wish to produce such a play? He said: "We must give them a novelty, something they cannot see in London." At my astonished query "They? Who?" he replied: "The English tourist." The producer thought I was little Stella. He couldn't believe I was seventy-four. But *Who's Who* has it correctly: *Born 9th February 1865*. I hope to get away to the South of France to a little hotel at the same price, but set in beauty— the lovely Ferme des Orangers with its nightingales, and the scent of the orange groves. I am getting used to poverty and discomfort, and even to the very real unhappiness of having no one to give me an arm when I cross the road carrying Moonbeam through the terrifying tearing traffic. Stella.

Lights begin a very slow dim on her.

SHAW. 4 Whitehall Court. 21st August 1939. My dear Stella: The giant is decrepit and his wife crippled with lumbago. Pascal wanted you for the part but he gave up because you would not be separated for six months from your dog. For Heaven's sake, when that wretched little animal perishes in the course of nature or is slain by an automobile, buy a giant panda or a giraffe or a water buffalo or a sea lion, any of which you can take with you anywhere. They make affectionate pets, though the water buffalo has a dangerous preference for black children. Cheetahs are real dears: I have petted one. [*Lights out on* CAMPBELL] I am keeping away from Malvern this year; but my new play has enlivened the Festival. It is all about Charles II, his wife, two of his whores, an actress, Isaac Newton, his housekeeper and housemaid, Kneller the painter, George Fox, the first Quaker, and James II (Duke of York in the play). [*Lights begin to fade*] I have given up producing; I am too old, too old, too old. G.B.S.

The "S" should be said in the dark.

Lights come up, the two rise in place, take Mss. up to hatbox, place them in it, close the lid.

Curtain

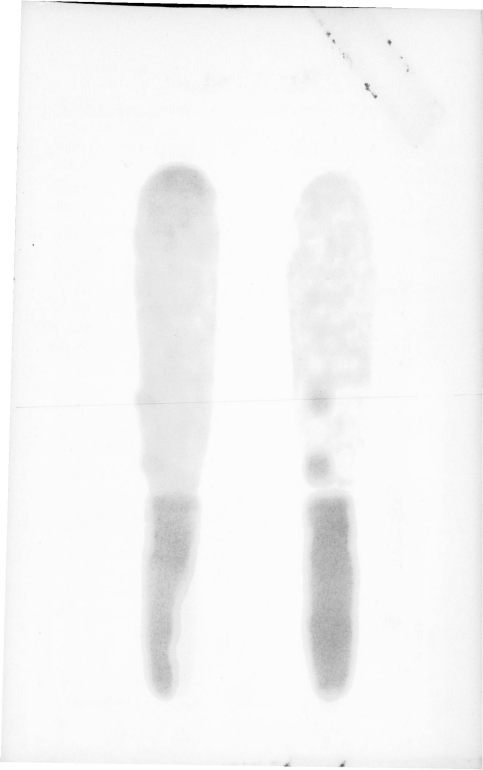

DATE DUE

GAYLORD   PRINTED IN U.S.A.